Pondering God

Craig McCourt

Blessings Tate
On your first mission adventure!
I know it will not be your last.
Heb. 13:16

Craig McCourt

John 20:31

DEDICATION

To my partner and bride, Shirley, who has inspired me to see God in the everyday and allowed me to share my stories with so many (even stories she has heard over and over and over and over…).

CONTENTS

ACKNOWLEDGMENTS

There have been many people over the years who have encouraged me to gather my GodPonders into a book. This is the result of their requests. While many of the ponders in this book are new, some are taken from my online blog collection written over the years. My blog can be found at GodPonders.org

My greatest acknowledgment needs to go to my Lord Jesus who has, through His living, breathing Word, given me so much to ponder.

PREFACE

*… they will **proclaim** the works of God and **ponder** what he has done.*
Psalm 64:9 (NIV)

For many years, the name of my online blog and speaking ministry has been "GodPonders." When people see that, they often ask "What does God Ponder?" The only answer I can come up with is, "nothing." God does not need to ponder anything. Has it ever occurred to you that nothing has ever occurred to God? No amount of thought or meditation is going to bring to God any new thoughts or ideas. Nothing we ever tell Him in prayer is going to surprise or stun Him. I believe in a God who is all-knowing, or omniscient. No room for pondering there.

I, on the other hand, often find myself knowing nothing, or "unniscient." (My little red squiggle appeared under unniscient; Microsoft Word has declared it to not be a word. Humph! It is now in print and I am sure it will soon be included in the Oxford Dictionary.)

Being unniscient, I have lots to ponder. But let me clarify, pondering is not the same as simply thinking. Pondering is the art of thinking, slowly, deliberately, and thoroughly to reach a conclusion. While many might say that pondering is a word that is out of favor, perhaps

1

too ancient, I say that it suits me just fine!

This book is a collection of GodPonders. These are the end results of taking time and pondering God. The hardest part of pondering God, for me, is to capture the GodPonder in writing. Because of the size, scope, and unfathomable nature of God, my pondering usually is this loosely connected series of thoughts, that lead to another series of thoughts, that lead to another . . .well, you get the point.

With that in mind, hats off to my editor, Melissa, who had to wade through all my rambling ponders and help others make sense of them—or at least make sure they won't cringe at my lack of grammar. I think it helps that she was once a former student of mine and has had years of trying to figure out what I am saying. In the spirit of full disclosure, English is my second language. The real trouble is that I do not have a first language.

As I ponder the finalizing of this book, I have one more item to clarify. Today, we in America are living in a post-Christian era. To include the word God in your title without the benefit of some clarification would be remiss.

When I speak about God, I am speaking about the one and only true God, the triune God who is Father, Son, and Holy Spirit. Three distinct persons in a single Godhead. I believe that the Father is the creator and sustainer of all life. I believe that He, the Son, and the Holy Spirit have existed from eternity and will be God through eternity. Tell me that doesn't give you something to ponder.

I believe that Jesus is the only unique son of God who was sent to Earth to live a perfect life and pay the total debt for my sin and yours by dying on the cross. I believe that, through His amazing resurrection from the dead after three full days, He has won my freedom from sin and death and the power of Satan over me.

I believe that I would not in the foggiest begin to understand any of this if it were not for the Holy Spirit who resides in me. This Spirit calls me, gathers me, and enlightens me on my journey through this earth.

I also believe that Jesus is the only way to the Father. I do not believe that all roads lead to God. I think the world tries to make us think that all roads of spirituality lead to God. Finally, I also believe that God allows much in this world that I do not understand, but His love and compassion for His people is unparalleled.

<>< Craig

The GodPonders mission: As disciples of Christ, we seek to use the stories of Scripture and life to proclaim the works of God and ponder what He has done, encouraging and equipping others to do the same.

NATIONAL CHEESECAKE DAY

Your love, O LORD, reaches to the heavens, your faithfulness to the skies.
Psalm 36:5 (NIV)

National Cheesecake Day is further proof of a divine creator. While National Cheesecake Day may not rank among the top American holidays, I feel it should be placed on the Christian calendar as a religious holiday. I'll explain this more in a moment.

Without a doubt, cheesecake is among my favorite desserts. My editor, Melissa, and her husband, Christian, had a cheesecake bar at their wedding reception several years ago, but my taste buds remember like it was just yesterday.

Let me back up and explain where my love of cheesecake comes from. My bride, Shirley, was looking through a collection of favorite dessert recipes from a magazine and she came upon a recipe for Triple Chocolate Cheesecake. For many years, while serving at Trinity in full-time youth ministry, we hosted a youth fundraiser called the Sweetheart Banquet. While the food was always tasty and the service was exceptional, I know why people really came. They came for the Triple Chocolate Cheesecake, homemade by my wife, Shirley.

It was while at Trinity that I had my first brush with diabetes, and my wife discovered that she could make a cheesecake that was still fantastic even with a sugar substitute. My addiction was born.

A few years later, Shirley picked up a cheesecake cookbook from the checkout aisle of a local grocery store. She then made it her mission to cook her way through the entire book—a mission I fully supported and encouraged. After all, a husband's job is to champion and encourage his wife in daily life and mission, right? We have had some amazing cheesecakes. White Chocolate Raspberry, Caramel Pecan, Pumpkin Swirl, and inevitably a couple of semi-duds (you can never have a total dud when it comes to cheesecake).

We have even hosted a National Cheesecake Day Party in our home, which featured a wide variety of cheesecakes for our guests. We have had people ask us when the next National Cheesecake Day Party is going to be. For the record, National Cheesecake Day is July 30, in case the publisher of your calendar did not choose to list it.

You know, if you need a moment to go get a piece of cheesecake, it's OK. I'll just wait here. You can come back and finish reading this later, maybe over a piece of cheesecake and a good cup of coffee. Coffee . . . oh, don't get me started.

Hey, you're back—awesome!

Now, to get back to why National Cheesecake Day should be a national Christian holiday. I don't know about you, but I enjoy food. I think most people do. I enjoy the wide variety of tastes and textures found in food. I enjoy the act of eating, both alone and even more so with others. Why? Why does food have so many tastes and textures? Was it necessary for God to put such a wide variety of tastes in the world? Was it necessary for Him to design a tongue, nose, and brain able to discern and enjoy them?

No, it was not, but God is good. The psalmist understood this when he spoke of this loving God with these famous words:

> *Taste and see that the LORD is good; blessed is the man who takes refuge in him.*
> Psalm 34:8 (NIV)

I have long been puzzled by these words. But I have grown to know that these words are literal. "Taste and see that the LORD is good." Every time we enjoy a new food or treat, it should cause us to pause and remember that our sense of taste was not a requirement, but a simple bonus from a God who loves us more than we can understand.

So are you with me? Will you add your name to the list of those who believe that National Cheesecake Day should be a national Christian holiday? We plan to celebrate it with cheesecake, scripture, and a time of grateful praise to a God who delights us.

SOMETHING TO PONDER:
What are some things that show you that God is good, and loves you more than you can imagine?

WRONG QUESTION

But these are written that you may believe that Jesus is the Christ, the Son of God, and that by believing you may have life in his name.
John 20:31 (NIV)

Many years ago, I had the chance to take a group of high school students to St. Petersburg, Russia on a short-term mission trip. It is a trip I reference often, for there is so much that I learned and observed while I was there. One of my favorite stories from that trip centers around a shopping trip that I took to a large market with a young man from my congregation, Sid. Sid was a great kid and a lot of fun to have along on the trip. Sid had followed most of the advice I had given prior to the trip, to help him prepare. I did say *most*; there was one simple piece of advice, however, that Sid chose to ignore. I encouraged Sid to learn just a few, simple Russian expressions, to show respect for the people and to help get around better while in the country.

Sid and I arrived at the market, which was a large, open-air market in a walled courtyard. The layout of the courtyard was a giant circle. Sid headed out one way and I headed the other. When I met up with Sid some time later, I had purchased many souvenirs, which was our mission on this day. Sid, by the time we connected, had purchased nothing. He said he was not able to buy anything because no one would talk to him. I explained that his English was not the language of the day here. Sid quickly wanted to learn a little Russian. I asked him what he wanted to learn how to say. His reply was quick, "'How much does this cost?' Teach me to say that." I asked him if he was sure that was what he wanted to learn. He was confident that phrase would make his shopping adventure a success. He was in luck—I was able, in my broken Texan/Russian, to tell him.

Delighted, he ran off to purchase all the things he had seen earlier. I followed at a distance to see how it was going. It was not long before he came back to see me. Turns out there was a problem. When he asked them, "How much does this cost?" they told him. In Russian. Deeply frustrated, he said, "this is not working at all." So I told him that it was a simple case of asking the wrong question. He was close with the question that he was asking, but something was still lacking. When we modified the question to, "How much does this cost, in English?" the results were very different.

The traders did not speak English, but they all had pocket calculators and they would simply type in a number and show you the price. The game then went on, and you would type a new number; this continued until you both came to a number you could live with. "How much does this cost?" seemed like the right question, but it never got to the real matter at hand.

That story sets up my next point. A movie played a few years ago on limited screens across the country, called *Oh My God*. It is a documentary from director Peter Rodger. *Oh My God* asks people from all walks of life—celebrities, religious, atheists, and the common man—the question, "What is God?"

I must admit, I have read reviews and watched a few clips from the movie, but have not seen the whole thing. But, even without watching it, I know that it suffers from the "wrong question dilemma." You see, the question is not, "What is God?" but, "Who is

God?". As scripture, creation, and the very heart of man all declare, God is not a "what" but a "who."

John opens his Gospel, the account of Jesus the Son of God come down to earth, with these words:

> *In the beginning was the Word, and the Word was with God, and the Word was God. He was with God in the beginning. Through him all things were made; without him nothing was made that has been made. In him was life, and that life was the light of men.*
> John 1:1-4 (NIV)

"He was with God in the beginning." "In him was life." John introduces his Lord to his reader not with a "what" but with a "who." Throughout the pages of scripture, God is defined in "person" terms. The trinity of God is revealed as Father, Son, and Holy Spirit, who are all listed as the "persons" of the Trinity.

John ends his Gospel with these words:

> *Jesus did many other miraculous signs in the presence of his disciples, which are not recorded in this book. But these are written that you may believe that Jesus is the Christ, the Son of God, and that by believing you may have life in his name.*
> John 20:30-31 (NIV)

Many might think I am getting overly picky here with the English language and the difference between "What is God?" and "Who is God?" but this language difference points out the underlying issues of our culture. Our culture today has ascribed, as did ancient pagan religions of the past, divine attributes and names to "stuff."

I put my hope in the "Who" that God is—Jesus the Christ. I believe that clearing up this distinction can make all the difference in the world in our daily walk with Christ. It reminds us that we are in a personal, intimate relationship with a living, loving God.

SOMETHING TO PONDER:
"What" is in your world that sometimes takes the place of "Who" God is?

I COULD SING OF YOUR LOVE FOREVER

Sing to the LORD a new song; sing to the LORD, all the earth.
Psalm 96:1 (NIV)

Yesterday I was listening to my iPod on the way home from work, set on "shuffle play." This gave me a good mix of my music as I traveled. About halfway home, I came upon a song that caught my ear. I will not share the title of the song, but I will tell you that, other than the words of the title, the song had very few lyrics. The title of the song was repeated for what seemed like a hundred times, one right after another, after another, after another, after another, after another. You get the point.

Some contemporary Christian artists have confused the title of a popular praise song, "I Could Sing of Your Love Forever" with the phrase, "I Should Sing of Your Love Forever." Now don't get me wrong, I think our lives should "sing" the praise of our God. But not always with words, and especially not always with the same words.

I think that sometimes we tend to live our lives like this. We glory in something wonderful that God has done for us, and then we spend the next year basking in the glow, singing the same chorus, all the while we remain where we are, unmoved and unchallenged. I know that God tells us to remember the things that He has done, and much

11

of the Old Testament is a constant retelling of the story of God. But I also know that God does not want us to just stagnate. He constantly calls us to new adventures, discoveries, and missions.

> *Show me your ways, O Lord, teach me your paths; guide me in your truth and teach me, for you are God my Savior, and my hope is in you all day long.*
> Psalm 25:4-5 (NIV)

The Bible is full of references to following after Christ, walking the path, with God as our guide. Movement—God calls us to be people on the move. Remembering and celebrating what He has done, while we move on to the next big adventure, the next stanza of our "song."

My prayer is that we would "Sing of Christ's Love Forever" with ever-changing verses added as we live and move through life with Him.

SOMETHING TO PONDER:
What song fits your journey today?

RIGHT ON THE TIP OF MY TONGUE

Not long ago, I had another random ponder. It should not surprise me anymore—most of my life is made up of random ponders. I had just walked into my favorite coffee shop, the Mocha Monkey, when I heard someone behind me say, "Oh, it is right on the tip of my tongue." This is an expression I have used myself many times. It does make me wonder where this phrase came from. After spending way too much time trying to Google for the answer to that question, here's what I found—I have no idea. What I do know is how frustrating it is to have the answer to a question or a name resting on the "tip of your tongue" and you cannot shake it loose.

> *Do not let this Book of the Law depart from your mouth; meditate on it day and night, so that you may be careful to do everything written in it. Then you will be prosperous and successful.*
> Joshua 1:8 (NIV)

After the death of Moses, Joshua was chosen to lead the people of God. He was also given advice from God on how to lead the people. He was told to not let the book of the Law depart from his mouth. Why? So he would be careful to do everything in it, thus finding himself prosperous and successful.

Did you notice the advice, "Do not let this Book of the Law depart from your mouth."? Mouth—not mind, not heart, but mouth. He calls us to speak the Word of God out loud to ourselves and to one another. Lately, I have been reading the Word of God out loud to myself and I must admit there is something powerful in engaging your entire body in the Word: your eyes to read it, your lips to speak it, and your ears to hear it.

So while I don't know where the phrase, "On the tip of my tongue" comes from, I pray that it has found new meaning—that the Word of God would find itself daily "on the tip of my tongue."

SOMETHING TO PONDER:
What Bible verse most frequently comes to the tip of your tongue?

THE FOLLOWING LEADER

When Jesus spoke again to the people, he said, "I am the light of the world. Whoever follows me will never walk in darkness, but will have the light of life."
John 8:12 (NIV)

It seemed like such a simple drive. A trip from Sherburn, Minnesota to Fairmont and back—just 15 miles each way. So, off I went to a meeting at St. Paul's Lutheran Church in Fairmont. It was a great winter morning for a drive. The roads were clear and the sun was shining. The meeting must have been very uneventful, because I cannot recall any details about it. The drive home, however, I will never forget.

The trip to St. Paul's took me about 15 minutes; of course, that was before the snow. I knew it was going to snow. In fact, it snowed through most of our meeting, and I watched the snow accumulating on the ground from the window of our meeting room. I kept an eye outside and thought, nothing to worry about yet; after all, it's only a 15-minute drive home.

By the time I got out to my car after my meeting, there were about four inches of snow on the ground, and it was coming down fast. Visibility was decent, so I headed through town back to the highway I had arrived on. The roads in town were snow-covered but still passable. Surely the interstate I-90 would be better than the city streets, I figured.

As I got closer to the freeway and more out in the open, I noticed that the wind was picking up. I slowly made my way onto the entrance ramp in what was nearing whiteout conditions. The good news was that I had plenty of time to get home. Using my best Minnesotan winter driving skills, I followed the car ahead of me, keeping their tail lights just in view. Before long, keeping them in view was forcing me to drive ever closer as the wind continued to blow. We were now driving just above an idle at about 5 miles per hour, but at least we were moving.

This continued for quite some time. As long as we were still moving, I knew we would be alright. I even checked the mileage so I'd know when I had to start watching for my exit in Sherburn. The last thing I needed would be to follow this guy to South Dakota. Gripping the steering wheel tightly (there's something about driving in a blizzard that makes you believe that the harder you grip the wheel, the better you can see), I continued on.

At some point, before we reached my exit, the car in front of me stopped. I stopped and waited. As I waited, I noticed there was a car behind me, following my tail lights as well. After what seemed like several minutes, someone knocked on my window. As I opened my window he said, "You can turn it off; we are going to be here a while." I asked him what had happened, and he invited me to get out and see for myself.

I got out and noticed the man in the car behind me doing the same. We started walking toward the front of the line of vehicles, including cars, pickups, and even semis. It took a while, but I soon discovered that we were not on I-90 anymore. We had turned off at the Welcome exit, halfway between Fairmont and Sherburn, and were now parked, one behind another, down the lane of a local farmer.

The truck in the front of that parade knew where he was going . . . Home! It is the rest of us who were just blindly following the car in front of us. So blindly that we didn't even notice the slow bank off the interstate or the long turn into the farm yard. We spent the next several hours in the home of the local resident, playing cards and drinking coffee. There were about 15 of us waiting until the wind died down enough for us to find our way back to the freeway.

There were a couple of lessons that I remember from that day. First, if you are following someone, you'd better be sure you know where they are headed! There are two kinds of poor leaders to watch out for. First, there are those who don't know that they are lost. They may be people with a heart of gold and who are full of great intentions, but if they are not following after Christ, we should not be following after them. Second, and more dangerous, are the people who are knowingly leading you astray. Scripture warns us that false prophets and deceivers will rise up among us. Even Satan, scripture tells us, will appear to us as an angel of light.

There are two words that Jesus repeated many times while on this earth: "Follow me." They are spoken with great love and compassion. He truly longs for those He comes in contact with to follow Him. He offers new life, hope, and purpose to those who will follow Him. Jesus promised His disciples, and still promises us today, that we do not need to wander around in the darkness. He said,

> "I am the light of the world. Whoever follows me will never walk in darkness, but will have the light of life"
> John 8:12 (NIV)

The second lesson I learned on that snowy day is that sometimes we are a leader and we don't even know it. The gentleman heading back to his farm had no idea that there was a parade of vehicles following him. I remember the first time my son repeated something he had seen or heard from me. It is a humbling experience to realize that

17

people are following you. Jesus calls us to "let your light shine before men, that they may see your good deeds and praise your Father in heaven" (Matthew 5:16). Jesus knows what we often forget—people are watching us. Maybe we need to turn around from time to time and see who is following us. Trust me when I tell you there is always someone following you. Where are you leading them?

As Christians, we are called to be both follower and leader. Paul embraced this dual role as he called the Corinthians to "Follow my example, as I follow the example of Christ" (1 Cor. 11:1). Now, before this dual role overwhelms you, let me tell you of a third lesson I learned that day. Following the one in front of you is easy, if you keep your eyes on them.

> *Let us fix our eyes on Jesus, the author and perfecter of our faith, who for the joy set before him endured the cross, scorning its shame, and sat down at the right hand of the throne of God. Consider him who endured such opposition from sinful men, so that you will not grow weary and lose heart.*
> Hebrews 12:2-3 (NIV)

SOMETHING TO PONDER:
Are you aware who is following you today?

LIGHT POLLUTION

When they saw the star, they were overjoyed.
Matthew 2:10 (NIV)

I have always thought the phrase "light pollution" was an interesting description of the abundance of light that large cities tend to give off. For several years, I worked in Edina, MN, an inner-ring suburb of Minneapolis, and I lived in Waconia, MN, an outer-ring suburb of Minneapolis. When I would drive home from work in the evenings, I could certainly understand the concept of light pollution. There were a few short miles of my drive that were almost completely dark except for the beams of my headlights, but even those "dark" miles had a "glow" in the sky from the lights of suburbia.

I still remember the first time I traveled to the Boundary Waters Canoe Area in northern Minnesota and, for the first time in my life, saw stars at night without the effect of "light pollution." It takes your breath away as you see a truly star-filled sky. I vividly remember the feeling that it would be possible to reach up and touch one of the stars.

Today, as I write, it is the Christian festival of Epiphany. It is the day we celebrate the coming of the magi to the home of Jesus the Christ, now a small child, and the revelation that the Messiah has come to save the nations. It is the day marked by a star, and the clear understanding of Jesus as the Light of the World. Those of you who know me well know that I am a BIG Epiphany fan. It is my favorite day of the year.

As I was reflecting this morning on my day and the Epiphany of Christ, the thought came to me that we suffer from two kinds of light pollution. We certainly suffer from a physical light pollution, but more problematic today is the fact that we suffer also from spiritual light pollution. There are so many things, ideas, and philosophies out there today that often make it difficult for us to see the Light of the World!

I pray that you would be given the eyes of Christ—holy "son-glasses" that would filter out all the light pollution of this world and help you to focus on Jesus the Christ, the Light of the World.

> *In the beginning was the Word, and the Word was with God, and the Word was God. He was with God in the beginning. Through him all things were made; without him nothing was made that has been made. In him was life, and that life was the light of men. The light shines in the darkness, but the darkness has not understood it. There came a man who was sent from God; his name was John. He came as a witness to testify concerning that light, so that through him all men might believe. He himself was not the light; he came only as a witness to the light. The true light that gives light to every man was coming into the world.*
> John 1:1-9 (NIV)

> *When Jesus spoke again to the people, he said, "I am the light of the world. Whoever follows me will never walk in darkness, but will have the light of life."*
> John 8:12 (NIV)

SOMETHING TO PONDER:
What "light" in your world is distracting you from Christ?

WHERE'S JESUS?

"Why were you searching for me?" he asked. "Didn't you know I had to be in my Father's house?"
Luke 2:49 (NIV)

Do you remember the popularity of the "Where's Waldo?" drawings? They were large drawings filled with lots of activity and crowded with people and animals. The idea was to spend time looking through the drawing for the elusive Waldo. He would be somewhere in the drawing, in his red-and-white striped shirt and stocking hat. For a time it seemed like we had nothing better to do than to look for the odd-looking boy in the striped stocking hat.

Luke also painted a picture for us of a scene with lots of activity and crowded with people and animals. It was the Passover, and the city of Jerusalem was packed to the gills with people and animals. After the festival was over, the faithful would gather for the journey home.

The pilgrims would almost always travel in large groups. There was safety in numbers, and it also made the trip home a more fun-filled adventure. The same was true for Jesus' family. Mary and Joseph had traveled to the festival with a large group of family and friends from the Nazareth area. This group knew each other well. Children would travel in packs among the caravan, playing games and running off the road from time to time, only to return to the safety of the group. These were cousins, friends, and neighbors.

The adults also journeyed in groups, families and friends talking about politics, religion, and the weather. Stories were being swapped and family history was being retold. Oral tradition was still a very big part of this culture. On this trip, like others, families often assumed the entire family was somewhere in the pack. Now it was time to check in, and Mary and Joseph could not seem to find Jesus. After a long, anxious search of the caravan, the decision was made to return to Jerusalem.

The anxiety must have been tremendous as they searched for a young Jewish boy among the masses of other young Jewish boys. There was no distinctive red-and-white stocking cap to look for this time. It must have been an exhausting search. What a relief it must have been to find Him sitting among a crowd, listening to the teachers in the temple.

Jesus told Mary that He was "about his Father's business." He was doing the work He was created for. This "Where's Jesus?" account causes me to ponder what business I am doing. I need to, perhaps, resolve to be about my Father's business. After all, I am certain that we are all hand-created by the Father and given certain gifts, abilities, and passions to serve and grow His Kingdom.

I believe that those gifts, talents, and passions are as mixed as our fingerprints. I also know that the Lord equips each church with the mix of gifts it needs to carry out the ministry of that congregation. So what does this mean for you and me? We all have our Father's business to carry out for the kingdom, whether our business is making coffee after church on Sunday morning, visiting those who are shut in, or leading a small-group Bible study.

Paul encourages us to be about our Father's business in whatever we do. He writes in Colossians,

> *And whatever you do, whether in word or deed, do it all in the name of the*
> *Lord Jesus,*
> *giving thanks to God the Father through him.*
> Colossians 3:17 (NIV)

So, if you are ever in the mood for a challenge and want to play "Where's Craig?" I pray that you will find me about my Father's business, no matter what I happen to be doing at the moment. In a perfect world, I will be in a room full of people, telling stories of how God continues to make Himself known in my life as I ponder the day-to-day events in my world. Just for the record, I will not be wearing a red-and-white striped "Waldo" hat. I will most likely be wearing a wire cross around my neck!

SOMETHING TO PONDER:
What business for His Kingdom has God created you to do?

IT ALL BEGAN WITH A PENCIL

I know what it is to be in need, and I know what it is to have plenty. I have learned the secret of being content in any and every situation, whether well fed or hungry, whether living in plenty or in want.
Philippians 4:12 (NIV)

D o you remember your first pencil? (Please say yes, so I don't feel so odd.) I do. While I don't remember the exact one, I remember it was one of those oversized giants that, as a young child, you can grip with your whole hand. I was excited just to have my own pencil, and so my fondness for office supplies was born. I loved my pencil, especially just after it was sharpened. But, in time, I wanted to be like my brothers.

They had the sleek, yellow #2 pencils with the fresh pink eraser on the top. I wanted one of those, mine now seemed babyish and clunky. It was full of teeth marks and the eraser had broken off some time ago. The day came, and I got my very own #2 special. Now I could use any pencil sharpener I wanted, not just the ones made for oversized, childish pencils. I even remember getting those topper erasers—now we were talking pencils! But then I found out there were mechanical pencils.

The mechanical pencils were cool-looking; they were clear so you could see the lead inside. And all you had to do was twist and new lead would appear. No more pencil sharpeners for me; no more standing in line for a turn at the sharpener, only to break the tip off as soon as you sat back down and started to write. Yes, the day came when I got my own mechanical pencils. Now I was set—I had found the Cadillac of pencils. But then I discovered that mechanical pencils came with thinner lead.

I was so done with the thick-leaded mechanical pencils; that was fine when I was first starting out, but I was a mechanical pencil expert by now. I moved on to the thin lead pencils that you didn't need to twist—you simply clicked and out came new lead. The erasers on these pencils were protected and kept from harm under a silver cap. After all, by this point in life who was making mistakes? Not me. But soon enough, we were allowed to use pens.

Pencils were so old-school . . . they were fine for a standardized test where we had to fill in the circle with our trusty #2 pencils. But pens were a sign of maturity and confidence, and so I found myself the proud owner of a Bic crystal pen—blue. These pens had a lifetime supply of ink in each one, or at least the lifetime of my pens. But in time I discovered pens that were erasable.

Erasable pens were the perfect pen. They had the nice flow of a ball point, but if a teacher changed their mind and you had to change something in your notes, you could. You now had the power to erase ink and not just scribble it out. Does it get any better than that? But soon I noticed the pen to top all pens.

One single pen that contained four different colors of ink, and it clicked—a fun rhythm instrument as well! Those were some geniuses that worked for Bic. Once I was sporting a Bic four-in-one pen I was the envy of everyone in the classroom, maybe even the world. It was the world's most perfect pen. But eventually I noticed markers. And not just any markers. Markers with scents.

Hello, Mr. Sketch scented markers. These markers were a treat, not only for the eye, but for the nose as well. Why not treat myself to a world of fresh fruit while drawing? The more senses that are involved in learning the better, that's just good educational practice. So these markers were not just a new desire of mine, they were for my educational good. But then I found highlighters.

The beauty of a highlighter was that you could use them to draw in blinding neon, plus you could use them to highlight text. Yet another educational need for a writing instrument. What better way to review my notes and my books than with a highlighter? The only downside of a highlighter was that they would bleed through the page, if I used them in my Bible. But in time I was given my first Bible Highlighter.

Don't even get me started on gel pens, or cross pens, pen sets or pens that even write while upside-down. Yes, I must confess I am a pen geek and my pen of choice today is a Uniball Jetstream 1.0 BLX series. While this stroll down memory lane was partially tongue-in-cheek, it is something I—and many of us—struggle with: discontentment. Even when, or perhaps especially when it comes to our stuff, we want the latest and greatest, the biggest, fastest, and most highly rated. We want to be early adaptors and will stand in line for days for a new phone.

Just to clear the record, I have never stood in line for a phone. My Nokia Windows phone is neither the latest or the greatest, unlike my pens. So what can we do about this lack of contentment? I have found the best cure for discontentment is to start a blessing list. Begin by writing down ten things for which you are thankful. Do this several days in a row—truth is, we could do it every day of the year and never run out of ideas.

We need to see ourselves for the blessed people we are. Not just for the material blessings we do or don't have, but for the mercy of God which is given to us fresh every morning.

Because of the LORD's great love we are not consumed, for his compassions never fail.
They are new every morning; great is your faithfulness.
I say to myself, "The LORD is my portion; therefore I will wait for him."
Lamentations 3:22-24 (NIV)

Do you see the Lord as your portion? I strive to know the contentment of Paul, who learned to be content in any and all circumstances. For me to know contentment is to know more and more of Christ, whose never-ending love and compassion for me go way beyond my circumstances and my stuff. He does not love me for what I have, but for who I am.

SOMETHING TO PONDER:
In what area of your life do you struggle with contentment?

I AM NOT ALONE

Ascribe to the LORD the glory due his name;
worship the LORD in the splendor of his holiness.
Psalm 29:2 (NIV)

B ack when I was in high school (1980 to be exact), our youth group took a road trip. This was quite an adventure for a ragtag youth group from Fond du Lac, Wisconsin. We traveled 1,021 miles in two days with an overnight stop at Concordia College in Seward, Nebraska. We were on our way to the first National Youth Gathering for the Lutheran Church—Missouri Synod, called "Rejoice in His Presence." I was very excited to be off on this adventure, but not so excited on day two, when the temperature of our bus kept getting warmer and warmer. We finally had to stop and get the AC looked at and repaired before we could be on our way.

We were "rejoicing in our AC" as our trip continued. All part of the adventure, the breaking down of our bus on that trip was the first of many bus/van incidents over my next 30 years. Great stories are built around these kinds of adventures, but this side trip had a cost. While the new AC was great, the simple fact was that we were going to get there behind schedule. Most of the rest of the details of that day escape me today, except for one.

By the time we made it to Moby Gym on the campus of Colorado State University, the opening night of the Gathering was already underway. We walked in on the middle of the opening worship service. What happened next I will never forget—we arrived in time to hear thousands (3-5 thousand if my memory serves me correctly) of youth praying the Lord's Prayer. It was an amazing experience. I had no idea that so many youth knew the Lord's Prayer. *WOW*, I thought, *look at all these Lutheran Christian youth!* I was not alone.

Since that time, I have had the experience of praying together with groups of up to 40,000 people, all celebrating the faith together. I truly am blessed by these experiences. There is something amazing that happens when God's people come together for worship. I worship now in a small church each Sunday morning I am not on the road, and there is something powerful in praying with the body of Christ in your own local church. To know most of the people in the room, and to know they are your neighbors and friends fills up my life on a weekly basis.

But there is another event that I remember. It, too, involved a trip with a group of people. Not a bus ride this time, but a plane ride to the Dominican Republic, followed by a long and bumpy bus ride— can't seem to shake those buses from my stories. But this time the event does not include a large group, although we did worship as a large group upon our arrival in the DR. This memory is of just two people, a small group—the smallest of groups, I suppose. This group was not in a gym or a sanctuary, but behind a small, humble home in La Cumbre, DR.

There was no formal worship service happening here, just a cement floor being laid in a form made from scrap wood (and even a tin can). The two people in this group didn't even speak the same language, on the outside. These two people took turns singing songs of praise to the Lord Jesus in two different spoken languages, but one language of the heart. This was worship at its finest. I am so blessed to have been a part of that remarkable worship event. I am grateful for the love and friendship born out of that event.

Who says worship only happens on Sunday? Who says worship only happens in a church? Know that we are not alone in this journey in faith we call life. Whenever you have the opportunity to sing, to pray, to ponder what God has done for you, whether in a small group or a large group, in a formal setting or in a backyard, make the most of it.

> *Let the word of Christ dwell in you richly as you teach and admonish one another with all wisdom, and as you sing psalms, hymns and spiritual songs with gratitude in your hearts to God.*
> Colossians 3:16 (NIV)

What a joy to travel this life in the presence of so many who speak our same heart language. I pray that you will know the joy of worship this week in the presence of a small group of people that you know and love. This journey of life was never intended for us to make alone. Be connected! Be blessed! Be encouraged as you encourage others.

SOMETHING TO PONDER:
Where do you like to worship?

THANKSGIVING IN THE DESERT

Give thanks in all circumstances, for this is God's will for you in Christ Jesus.
1 Thessalonians 5:18 (NIV)

I cannot begin to know what it must have been like for the children of Israel to wander for 40 years in the desert. I do, however, know something about life in the desert. Now, I'm not talking about the dry, sandy area full of cacti and snakes that we call a desert.

I'm talking about the part of the journey of life where we seem to be wandering and lost. It's those moments when you seem to have more questions for God than answers, when your passion seems stifled. Those times when the future looks so uncertain and unknown. Perhaps for you it is the desert of job loss, financial issues, health, or even grief.

I have to admit, as I write this GodPonder I find myself in the desert. There are days when it is a struggle to make ends meet. I feel called and gifted by God to tell His story to others, but opportunities seem few and far between. We just laid my dad's ashes in their final resting place, after his death this summer, as I watch my mom enter hospice care. We received the sad news of the death of Shirley's brother, which happened while he was on vacation with his wife in Spain.

On this Thanksgiving day, the words of Paul echo in my mind and they come to me as a comfort, a reminder of the steady, constant love of God. Paul not only calls us to give thanks, but I think he reminds us we *can* give thanks in all circumstances. Want me to start listing my blessings? I would miss worship this morning and turkey this afternoon if I listed them all. I do know I am blessed to be here, sitting in my office, on my computer, in my home, as the final preparations for a family gathering are being made.

As an avid amateur photographer, I love to take photos of God's creation. I can't tell you how long it took me to decide on a cover photo for this book. I looked through more than a thousand photos I had taken. I picked one of the most recent photos I had taken, from my most recent trip to Arizona to lay Dad's ashes to rest. I spent some time trying to capture a sunset in the desert. The photo on the cover is from that series, called *Desert of Life*.

> *And this is what he promised us—even eternal life.*
> 1 John 2:25 (NIV)

Eternal life—not eternal wandering—is the gift of God by grace through the love and sacrifice of Jesus Christ my Lord! This is most certainly true.

SOMETHING TO PONDER:
What makes you thankful today?

MEMORY ISSUES

But God remembered Noah and all the wild animals and the livestock that were with him in the ark, and he sent a wind over the earth, and the waters receded.
Genesis 8:1 (NIV)

We all have them—those moments where we simply forget. As I sat down to write today's post, I realized just how dusty my keyboard was. I got up from my desk and walked out to the garage to get a can of compressed air. (We all know that posts are better when typed with a clean keyboard.) Somewhere between the office and the garage, the idea completely left my mind. I stood by my workbench for about ten seconds, realizing that I was not going to will myself to remember.

So, I grabbed the superglue on my bench and went back into the house to fix my wife's teapot. Having successfully glued the handle back on the lid, I returned to my keyboard. Once I sat down, I realized just how dusty my keyboard was. I got up from my desk and walked out to the garage to get a can of compressed air. I returned, triumphant, with a can of compressed air. As you can tell from my typing, my keyboard is now much cleaner.

I have acquired a number of memory issues over the years. I have been known to call my own office phone and leave myself a message.

I have set random, odd objects on my front seat in the car to remind me about something I wanted to do the next time I got into my car. I have used a Franklin, even before Franklin met Covey. I have used a digital voice recorder. I have used a long list of productivity and list-making apps. These things all work in various forms and for various reasons.

Today, I was reading the familiar account from Genesis 6-9 of Noah and the great flood. In the reading today, I discovered something I had not seen before in my 52 years of life. (Unless I forgot it.) When Noah leaves the ark, along with all the animals and his family, God makes a covenant with Noah.

> *Then God said to Noah and to his sons with him: "I now establish my covenant with you and with your descendants after you and with every living creature that was with you—the birds, the livestock and all the wild animals, all those that came out of the ark with you—every living creature on earth. I establish my covenant with you: Never again will all life be destroyed by the waters of a flood; never again will there be a flood to destroy the earth."*

> *And God said, "This is the sign of the covenant I am making between me and you and every living creature with you, a covenant for all generations to come: I have set my rainbow in the clouds, and it will be the sign of the covenant between me and the earth. Whenever I bring clouds over the earth and the rainbow appears in the clouds, I will remember my covenant between me and you and all living creatures of every kind. Never again will the waters become a flood to destroy all life. Whenever the rainbow appears in the clouds, I will see it and remember the everlasting covenant between God and all living creatures of every kind on the earth."*
> Genesis 9:8-16 (NIV)

It struck me, while reading this passage, that the rainbow serves as a reminder to God. While I know that it is a sign to us as well, He speaks of it as a reminder for Him. As I ponder this, I'm struck by the fact that God watches us closely enough to catch the fleeting rainbows that follow a storm. What a wonderful thought: that God not only is present in the storm, but is with us after the storm and enjoys the rainbow along with us.

Since I also am well aware of God's ability to remember what He chooses, and forget what He chooses, I'm glad He remembers His promises. He has marked so much of our daily life with reminders of His presence. As I write, looking out my office window on a beautiful fall day, I'm reminded by the amazing yellows and reds of this season of the joy God puts into our everyday life!

SOMETHING TO PONDER:
How has God reminded you of His presence today?

LESSONS FROM LAMBEAU

I recently went to my first regular season game at historic Lambeau Field in Green Bay, WI. As a life-long Packers fan, this was a treat. A beautiful September day, with temperatures in the mid 60s, with 78,000 rabid Packers fans and a smattering of 14 Jets fans, 3 confused Vikings fans, and 1 Bears fan made for a great day. Having the Packers win the game made the day even better. But this was no ordinary game.

After a fumbled snap on the first play of the game, the Jets were off to the races, racking up the points to a 21-3 lead over the Packers late in the second quarter. The game was not even half over when this crowd seemed to turn on their beloved Packers. (Though disappointed, this author was quoted saying, "It's only the second quarter, and these are the Packers!")

I was somewhat stunned by the reaction of the crowd. Several fans seated directly behind me left Lambeau, never to return. (Thanks, by the way—we could spread out a little more and we enjoyed that!) These fans, many of whom had paid hundreds of dollars to get into the game, wearing hundreds of dollars worth of team jerseys and cheese, were ranting at their team. As if expecting nothing short of perfection from a group of athletes who collectively have a long history of personal failures.

"You're playing against a college offense and this is the best you can do?" . . . "Would it kill you to run the ball?" . . . "Why would you ever choose to run the ball?" . . . "I've seen better football at a high school game." . . . and these are just a few of the comments I can repeat here.

This all started to turn around in the final two minutes of the first half, as the Packers launched a very "Packers-like" comeback. The mood of the fans quickly changed and they were soon cheering for their team once again. "Now that's the way we play football!" . . . "Oh yeah, bring it on!" . . . "Go – Pack – Go!" Even the "wave" started around the stadium.

What changed? The players on the field were the same, the weather had not changed, they were not distributing free food or beverage— so what changed? The fans were getting what they wanted. I believe today there are way too many "fans" of Jesus and His church, and not enough "followers" or "disciples." Many times, I fall into a fan mentality with an attitude of, "What have you done for me lately?" To be a follower of Christ genuinely calls us to suffer with Him at times, that we might share in His glory!

Now if we are children, then we are heirs—heirs of God and co-heirs with Christ, if indeed we share in his sufferings in order that we may also share in his glory.
Romans 8:17 (NIV)

Sometimes God does not do what I want Him to; sometimes He disciplines me, and challenges me to simple obedience. Spoiler alert: if you read the end of the book (Revelation)—We win! Christ and His Church 1,000,000 – Satan 0.

Trust me when I say that sitting with your family on a beautiful September day in Green Bay, even when the Pack is not playing well

against the Jets, is not suffering! (Now watching the Vikings play . . .
well . . .)

SOMETHING TO PONDER:
In what way are you a "fair weather fan" of Jesus?

THE FEEDING OF THE 5,000 (MINUS 4,998)

You open your hand and satisfy the desires of every living thing.
Psalm 145:16 (NIV)

I found something else I have in common with the disciples. I, too, suffer from short-term memory loss. I like to think my case is not as severe as the disciples, but the truth is I think that mine is worse.

In chapter 9 of Luke's Gospel, Jesus sends out His disciples to proclaim the kingdom of God. That is just what they did. They preached good news, healed the sick, and sent demons on the run. After hearing about the beheading of John, they returned and, together with Jesus, tried to find a little solitude.

> *When the apostles returned, they reported to Jesus what they had done. Then he took them with him and they withdrew by themselves to a town called Bethsaida, but the crowds learned about it and followed him. He welcomed them and spoke to them about the kingdom of God, and healed those who needed healing.*
> Luke 9:10-11 (NIV)

It sounded like a good idea—to withdraw and get a little rest—but it was not to be. The crowds found them. So Jesus did what Jesus does: He welcomed them and spoke to them about the kingdom of God, and healed those who needed healing. I am sure the crowd just continued to swell all day.

The disciples then sensed a problem: these people were going to get hungry. They also sensed a solution: Jesus should send them away. Late in the afternoon the Twelve came to Him and said,

> *"Send the crowd away so they can go to the surrounding villages and countryside and find food and lodging, because we are in a remote place here."*
> Luke 9:12 (NIV)

It seemed like a reasonable solution, didn't it? . . . or did it? I believe they were suffering from short-term memory loss. This was Jesus—the one who had taught them and empowered them to go on their first short-term mission trip. This was Jesus—the one who casts out demons, heals the sick, and gives sight to the blind. This was Jesus—who seemed to always be three steps ahead of the disciples.

Where was their confidence in God's ability to provide for them? Their first step was spot on—they came to Jesus with their concern. But this is where the disciples and I are so alike. Rather than just leaving the concern there, and trusting that Jesus would deal with it, they started making suggestions about how to best deal with the situation.

How many times does God need to prove Himself faithful in my life before I stop bringing my needs, along with my suggested solutions to Him? Haven't I, like the disciples, seen Jesus work miracles? Yet I still, at times, think that the Lord needs a few fresh ideas about how to deal with the situations in my life.

While having trouble making ends meet with our mortgage, I had a solution for the Lord. "Let's sell the house and move to a smaller townhome," I told Him. How did that suggestion work out? We had over fifty showings and not a single offer. OK, so maybe the Lord had a better plan. So now I sit here, having witnessed the feeding of the 5,000 (minus 4,998) as God "daily and richly provides all that I need to support this body and life" (Martin Luther).

SOMETHING TO PONDER:
How has God demonstrated His provision in your life?

MRI PONDERS

The Word became flesh and made his dwelling among us.
We have seen his glory, the glory of the One and Only, who came from the Father,
full of grace and truth.
John 1:14 (NIV)

I have had many cervical MRIs—one of the joys of a (literal) pain in the neck. During one MRI in particular, they asked me all the usual questions designed to make sure that no metal planted in my body would be pulled out by the magnetic field of the machine. They asked me to describe the symptoms I was having. They asked about my height and weight. They asked, "What do you want to listen to while you are having the procedure?" Their final question was my favorite, "Are you claustrophobic?" I replied, "We'll soon find out."

I then explained to the technician that I had never had a serious issue with an MRI. Don't get me wrong, they are not my favorite test in the world. It does, however, rank higher than a colonoscopy or the dreaded "bite-wing x-rays."

While I was trying to focus on listening to the Christian music channel I had selected, I heard a familiar Chris Tomlin song: "Indescribable." As I pondered the indescribable nature of God, I remembered the last question they asked me. Do you remember what it was? "Are you claustrophobic?"

> *He (Jesus) is the image of the invisible God, the firstborn over all creation. For by him all things were created: things in heaven and on earth, visible and invisible, whether thrones or powers or rulers or authorities; all things were created by him and for him. He is before all things, and in him all things hold together. And he is the head of the body, the church; he is the beginning and the firstborn from among the dead, so that in everything he might have the supremacy. For God was pleased to have all his fullness dwell in him, and through him to reconcile to himself all things, whether things on earth or things in heaven, by making peace through his blood, shed on the cross.*
> Colossians 1:15-20 (NIV)

Jesus was not claustrophobic. To have all the fullness of God reside in a human form would be the ultimate test of claustrophobia. I recall the classic line from the Disney movie, *Aladdin*, when the genie gives a brief summary of life as a genie: "Ultimate cosmic power, itty-bitty living space."

I am in awe of Christ, who took on the constraints of human form for me—I was only confined in the MRI for what amounted to about thirty minutes. Next time you get a little feeling of claustrophobia— perhaps from a cubical at work, an elevator ride, a packed airplane, or while trying to figure out where to store all your "stuff" in your new, smaller home—take a moment for a GodPonder.

> *Your attitude should be the same as that of Christ Jesus: Who, being in very nature God, did not consider equality with God something to be grasped, but made himself nothing, taking the very nature of a servant, being made in human likeness. And being found in appearance as a man, he humbled himself and became obedient to death— even death on a cross!*
> Philippians 2:5-8 (NIV)

SOMETHING TO PONDER:
What moments have helped you get a better perspective on God?

THE "EAT MORE—GAIN MORE" DIET

He humbled you, causing you to hunger and then feeding you with manna,
which neither you nor your fathers had known,
to teach you that man does not live on bread alone
but on every word that comes from the mouth of the LORD.
Deuteronomy 8:3 (NIV)

I just stepped off the scale and once again reminded myself of the simple truth that my weight is not a constant. It changes on a daily basis. Sometimes the number goes down, most of the time it goes up, but it rarely stays the same. I was also reminded that it is time I put a little effort into making it go down.

I remember my college roommate's first attempt at weight loss. He had heard, like so many of us, that salads were a good source of nutrition, and great for a diet. So he proceeded to add a salad to lunch and dinner each day. He did not replace the entrée or the dessert with a salad—he simply added a salad to the mix. Needless to say, he did not lose any weight.

One of the simple axioms of life is, "Eat Less—Lose Weight." Now, we also know that the converse is true: "Eat More—Gain Weight." If you don't believe me, I can submit lots of personal testimony to this simple fact.

As I was pondering the Word this morning, this familiar verse stood out to me:

Taste and see that the LORD is good; blessed is the man who takes refuge in him.
Psalm 34:8 (NIV)

I don't think the psalmist was talking about a new diet plan. I do, however, wonder if I put as much effort into my spiritual diet as I do my physical diet. I started pondering . . . What does my diet of the Word look like? Am I eating just enough to survive? Am I just in "maintenance mode," trying to maintain my spiritual weight? Or am I bulking up? Am I feasting on the Word so that I will be ready, strong, and prepared for daily life?

What if we put as much effort into our spiritual diet as our physical diet? It is a rare day that I miss a meal, or even an evening snack. When I am being deliberate about my eating habits, I can be downright militant about what and when I eat. Why, then, do I find it so challenging to keep this same routine in the Word?

Another tried and true fact about weight loss is that exercise helps you lose more fat and gain muscle. James explains spiritual exercise: the simple fact that hearing the Word needs to followed by acting on the Word.

Do not merely listen to the word, and so deceive yourselves. Do what it says.
James 1:22 (NIV)

Research has also shown that dieting works best when it is done along with a level of accountability. You will be more successful in dieting when you have someone with whom you can share your struggles and victories. In our spiritual fitness program, we have two levels of accountability and support. The first level is with our coach, through prayer. The designer, creator, and sustainer of life wants nothing more than to support, encourage, and advise you in your journey. The second level of accountability is with the body of Christ. Find a body of believers with whom you can study the Word, discuss it, and live it out!

SOMETHING TO PONDER:
What does your diet of the Word look like?

SOMETHING TO TALK ABOUT

A good name is more desirable than great riches; to be esteemed is better than silver or gold.
Proverbs 22:1 (NIV)

I t was one of the first days of the year that I could drive with my windows down. What a glorious day. One of the joys of this kind of day is being able to blare your music for all the world to hear. One of the troubles of this kind of day is having to listen to the music as everyone else also blares their music. That day, as I waited at a red light, I was treated to a song that got stuck in my head. For the rest of the day, I was unable to get it unstuck.

The song is not on any of my playlists, I have none of her albums in my collection of 1,000+ CDs. It was stuck in my head nonetheless. The song, as you may have guessed from the title above, is "Something to Talk About," by Bonnie Raitt (off her 1991 album *Luck of the Draw*). The premise of the song is that people are gossiping about two other people. They are talking about a relationship that they believe exists between them, based on what they are seeing:

People are talkin', talkin' 'bout people,
I hear them whisper, you won't believe it.
They think we're lovers kept under cover,

I just ignore it but they keep sayin' we…
Laugh just a little too loud,
Stand just a little too close,
We stare just a little too long.

The chorus goes on to invite the second person in this story to consider an intimate relationship.

Let's give 'em somethin' to talk about
(Somethin' to talk about)
Let's give 'em somethin' to talk about
(Somethin' to talk about)
Let's give 'em somethin' to talk about
How about love?

This song got me pondering . . . Do people start rumors about me? What are they saying about me? Do they see me living my relationship with Christ out loud? Does it make them wonder what's going on in my life? I hope so. I think that is what Jesus meant when He told us to shine.

> *In the same way, let your light shine before men, that they may see your good deeds and praise your Father in heaven.*
> Matthew 5:16 (NIV)

Sometimes I think our witness gives people plenty to talk about when our words *don't* meet our actions. That is not the witness we need them talking about. As fallen people who make mistakes, we can live lives that seek and share forgiveness. This will *really* give them something to talk about.

I think, perhaps, the chorus of this song should find its way into a hymn, a rally cry for the church to stand up and be noticed. Noticed for the joy of the Lord in the midst of our tears, for our peace that comes from Christ in the midst of fear, and the compassion of our

49

God in a world full of suffering. Maybe it could look something like this:

....they keep sayin' we...
Laugh just a little too loud,
Shine just a little too bright,
We serve just a little too much.

Let's give 'em somethin' to talk about
(Somethin' to talk about)
Let's give 'em somethin' to talk about
(Somethin' to talk about)
Let's give 'em somethin' to talk about
How about love?

Let's start some rumors by living lives that demand explanation.

P.S. Be careful what song you crank on your car radio . . . you never know who might be listening.

SOMETHING TO PONDER:
What would people say about the way you live your life?

AT THE MONKEY

Every good and perfect gift is from above, coming down from the Father of the heavenly lights, who does not change like shifting shadows.
James 1:17 (NIV)

For many years, my weekly routine included a scheduled day during which I would write a new GodPonder. Many of those early ponders were written from my all-time favorite coffee shop, The Mocha Monkey, in Waconia, MN. What makes it a great coffee shop? Good question . . . I guess it is the combination of good coffee, a friendly atmosphere, and the comfort of the familiar.

In a world of high-speed change, constant mobility, and fast-paced everything, it is nice to spend a little time in the familiar. That got me thinking—or should I say pondering—what else in my life I would consider familiar. Shirley and I are friends with a group of couples that we have known for years, and with whom we have grown close. We are all about the same age, our kids went through school together, and we all raised our kids in the same church. They are familiar. There is something very comfortable about talking with them.

Familiarity—I long for it at times. I live in a new home (we've been here for less than two years), in a new community, with a new day job (pencil salesman), while launching a new ministry. So I rejoice in my

51

family—my familiar—enjoying the company of my wife of 27 years, attending a Timberwolves game with my 22-year-old, and spending an evening phone call discussing politics with my 19-year-old.

But more than anything I treasure my familiar faith in my familiar Lord. The unchanging God who has been walking with me as long as I can remember, even when I was unaware of it. The familiar hymns of my youth sung in worship, the familiar praise choruses I sang with my kids for years. His familiar Word speaks volumes to me. It is a comfort for me to read words that I have turned to for years.

So I find comfort in my familiar coffee shop, with my familiar Bible.

> *Do you not know? Have you not heard? Has it not been told you from the beginning? Have you not understood since the earth was founded?*
> Isaiah 40:21 (NIV)

Since the earth was formed . . . that's a long time. Our God is a God of the familiar. When we turn to Him we recognize Him—His voice is familiar.

> *Do you not know? Have you not heard? The LORD is the everlasting God, the Creator of the ends of the earth. He will not grow tired or weary, and his understanding no one can fathom.*
> Isaiah 40:28 (NIV)

He will not grow weary . . . I am familiar with weariness and love a God who never suffers from it!

> *He gives strength to the weary and increases the power of the weak. Even youths grow tired and weary, and young men stumble and fall; but those who hope in the LORD will renew their strength. They will soar on wings like eagles; they will run and not grow weary, they will walk and not be faint.*
> Isaiah 40:29-31 (NIV)

These are perhaps the most familiar words of the Bible to me. They are words I turn to over and over, they are words I have called my favorite for years. What is familiar in your life? What do you hang on to, and return to, for that comfortable feeling of familiarity?

If your life is feeling rushed, changing drastically, or if you are feeling like you are always on the edge of a steep learning curve, then take some time and spend it with the familiar. Spend some time with our familiar and faithful God.

SOMETHING TO PONDER:
What feels familiar to you? What is your most familiar Bible verse?

SONG OF THE SAINTS

Sing to him a new song; play skillfully, and shout for joy.
Psalm 33:3 (NIV)

All Saints Day is a day where we, the church on Earth, remember and celebrate the Church Triumphant. The song of the saints here in the earthly kingdom of God's grace joins with the song of the saints in the heavenly kingdom of glory. As I reflect on that great celebration, a question comes to mind: What song do you sing?

The song of the saints is not the song that the world so often sings: "Salvation belongs to those who look good." Scripture reminds us that, while man looks at the outward edge of a man, the Lord searches the heart. Salvation does *not* belong to those who look good in the world's eyes.

> *But the LORD said to Samuel, "Do not consider his appearance or his height, for I have rejected him. The LORD does not look at the things man looks at. Man looks at the outward appearance, but the LORD looks at the heart."*
> 1 Samuel 16:7 (NIV)

Many would say, "Amen," to the statement above. Their song says, "Salvation belongs to those who act good." They recognize that outward beauty has nothing to do with it; you must have "good" actions. Letting the world see the "good" side of you. But salvation does *not* belong to those who act "good."

> *"Be careful not to do your 'acts of righteousness' before men, to be seen by them. If you do, you will have no reward from your Father in heaven. "So when you give to the needy, do not announce it with trumpets, as the hypocrites do in the synagogues and on the streets, to be honored by men. I tell you the truth, they have received their reward in full.*
> Matthew 6:1-2 (NIV)

Still more will join in with strong support that this second song is also not the song of the saints. Their song—perhaps the most dangerous song of all—sings that "Salvation belongs to those who *are good.*" They strive, perhaps with great sincerity, to do good and earn the favor of God. Scripture also reminds us that there is no one who is good, there is no one without sin.

> *For all have sinned and fall short of the glory of God.*
> Romans 3:23 (NIV)

Here, too, they have missed the song of the saints—their song is filled with striving, serving, and false hope. Paul has more to say to us in this section of Romans.

> *This righteousness from God comes through faith in Jesus Christ to all who believe. There is no difference, for all have sinned and fall short of the glory of God, and are justified freely by his grace through the redemption that came by Christ Jesus.*
> Romans 3:22-24 (NIV)

So what is the song of the saints? What do they sing, gathered in an unnumbered crowd before the throne of God? In St. John's book of Revelation we hear about the song of the saints.

Scripture makes clear what song the saints sing around the throne.

> *And they cried out in a loud voice: "Salvation belongs to our God, who sits on the throne, and to the Lamb."*
> Revelation 7:10 (NIV)

My prayer is that we all stop singing the songs of this world and start to sing the true song of the saints. I want to close by asking you to take a few minutes and break into song. Spontaneously worship the God who freely gives His salvation to you and me. Remember, He does this not because we look good, or act good, or even are good (because we are not). Salvation is ours because GOD IS GOOD. He has given His one and only Son for us, that salvation might be ours!

SOMETHING TO PONDER:
What hymn would you love to sing around the throne?

TEACH US TO...

Very early in the morning, while it was still dark, Jesus got up, left the house and went off to a solitary place, where he prayed.
Mark 1:35 (NIV)

There was a group of men, hand-picked by Jesus, known as the disciples. This band of merry men spent the bulk of three years with Jesus. They traveled from place to place with Him. They ate with Him, listened to Him, watched Him, touched Him, and knew Him better than anyone else on Earth.

John, a disciple of Jesus, became a part of the inner circle of three disciples: Peter, James, and John. John opened his first letter to the church with these words:

That which was from the beginning, which we have heard, which we have seen with our eyes, which we have looked at and our hands have touched--this we proclaim concerning the Word of life. The life appeared; we have seen it and testify to it, and we proclaim to you the eternal life, which was with the Father and has appeared to us. We proclaim to you what we have seen and heard, so that you also may have fellowship with us. And our fellowship is with the Father and with his Son, Jesus Christ. We write this to make our joy complete.
1 John 1:1-4 (NIV)

Can you sense John's excitement? He did not just hear about Jesus—
he heard directly from Him, he saw Him face to face, and he touched
Him. I know I would be excited to share these events. The disciples
were the first line of witnesses to all that Jesus said and did. As
disciples, they were students of Jesus the Rabbi. They learned much
from Him in the three years they spent together.

Imagine all they learned just by watching Jesus do the miraculous.
They saw Him change water to wine. They were there when the
outcasts of society, the lepers, were cleansed of their disease. They
experienced His command over nature, as even the wind and waves
obeyed His commands. They rejoiced with the mother whose son
returned from the dead at the request of Jesus. They were there with
the thousands who spent the day listening to Him. They observed
His ability to silence the criticism of the religious leaders with just a
simple question.

Of all the things these disciples witnessed, we only hear about them
requesting once for Jesus to teach them. What did they want to know
how to do? To raise the dead? To give sight to the blind? To multiply
food? To command the wind?

No. The disciples didn't ask for any of the big things that would
come to our minds after reading the gospel of Christ. Luke records
their one request of Jesus.

> *One day Jesus was praying in a certain place. When he finished, one of his
> disciples said to him, "Lord, teach us to pray, just as John taught his
> disciples."*
> Luke 11:1 (NIV)

Did you catch it? They asked Him to teach them to pray. Jesus'
example of prayer left the biggest impression with them of all He had
done. Prayer is the one thing they wanted to learn how to do like
Jesus. They had seen Him pray. They had seen his connection to the

Father. They saw this amazing ability to keep ministering whenever the time presented itself. They wanted that peace, that connection.

SOMETHING TO PONDER:
What do you want Jesus to teach you? (Go ahead and ask Him!)

71 WORDS

He said to them, "When you pray, say:
'Father, hallowed be your name, your kingdom come.'"
Luke 11:2 (NIV)

I've discovered that it often does not take a lot of words to get a response from people. "The Packers are in first place," or "The Vikings are in a building year," are just a few examples. Sometimes just a few words can have a life-changing effect on us. "It's a boy!" or, "It's cancer." Sometimes it takes a lot of words—the reading of an article, or a book—to change our perspective on an issue or make a change in our life.

Today I want to recommend 71 words. Words that, on most days, do not rock your world, or even illicit much of a response. The words are well-known; in fact, I could hazard a guess and say you know them already. Today, I want you to read the 71 words slowly, one at a time, and let them sink in. Are you ready?

"Our Father, who art in heaven, hallowed be Thy name,
Thy kingdom come, Thy will be done on earth as it is in heaven.
Give us this day our daily bread; and forgive us our trespasses
as we forgive those who trespass against us; and lead us not into
temptation, but deliver us from evil. For Thine is the kingdom
and the power and the glory for ever and ever. Amen."

This collection of 71 words should be enough to rock your world. They should be enough to cause a reaction, and empower a change. These words are so full of power, meaning, and life . . . it is a shame that we speed through them most of the time without even fully engaging our brain.

Many years ago, while serving a congregation in Milwaukee, I led a weekly Bible study for the residents of a Bethesda group home the church partnered with. There are many fun stories from those days of ministry with the dear saints in the group home. I am forever grateful to one of those residents, whose name was Mary.

At the end of each Bible class we would, as a group, close our prayer time with the Lord's Prayer. On this particular night, I was not paying a lot of attention to my own words. I don't remember the specific order to my words, but I will never forget that I got "power," "kingdom," and "glory" mixed up.

As soon as the mistake was clear of my lips, Mary jumped up and began to run around the table, crying, "oh no, oh no." When I eventually got her calmed down, I asked her what had happened. With a trembling voice, she explained quietly, so no one else could overhear, "You messed up the LORD'S PRAYER. It's the Lord's Prayer, you are in trouble, this is HIS prayer." She was gravely concerned for my wellbeing. I'm fairly certain that, in her mind, my very salvation at that moment was in question.

I was able to reassure Mary, and we as a group prayed the prayer again—correctly! That was more than thirty years ago, but I still like to have those 71 words in front of me as I speak them.

What began as a practice to never jeopardize my salvation again ended with a desire to take the words seriously. Following the text helps me to better ponder what I am saying.

So, all you worship leaders out there, let's slow it down a bit . . . we are not at the Kentucky Derby when we pray. If not for me, slow down for the little children of the congregation who are trying to pray along but haven't yet mastered speed praying . . . let's ponder every word!

SOMETHING TO PONDER:
Which of the 71 words of the Lord's Prayer are most meaningful to you today?

NEW MATH

You open your hand and satisfy the desires of every living thing.
Psalm 145:16 (NIV)

Math is not my best subject. If you have read my blog for long you might say, "Funny . . . I thought grammar and spelling were not his best subjects." Now you know why I am a public speaker first, a business person second, and a writer third.

Many times during my educational career, I complained about my inability to do math. I would blame my "not getting it" on "that darn new math." To this day, I tend to estimate low; running numbers in my head is just not safe—it tends to leave me two boards short of finishing the project or two feet short of where it needs to go. There are witnesses to this fact: those who went with me on a mission trip to West Virginia a few years ago.

On the last day of the trip, using our last 4x4, I cut the final corner support post for the back porch of a house we were working on. Somehow, the post shrank from when I cut it until when I tried to put it in place. When the post was held into place, it was obvious to everyone that new math had struck again . . . the post was six inches too short. I thought maybe I had grabbed the wrong end of the cut 4x4, only to discover that the other end was several feet too short.

I believe that once again, just like that experience, I am being hung up by new math. Dealing with depression on a good day can, at times, become a challenge. When the new math of the family finances does not seem to be working out, however, I now know it is old math I am suffering from. The disciples also suffered from old math. At the feeding of the 5,000, they came up with 5+2=7. They knew that five loaves of bread and two fish did not equal enough to feed all the hungry mouths on that hillside. The good news is, they knew who to tell about the problem—Jesus.

I have wondered if the Lord was really talking to ME when He led us to launch GodPonders. The old math was just not adding up. The phone was not ringing off the hook, and the money we had was running out the door. I began to think about how I could fix this situation. I started to make plans; perhaps a call back into the parish would be the best way. Maybe selling the house and buying something smaller would be the best. Getting a better job could be the solution, or maybe Amway. (Actually, Amway has never come to mind.)

I realized that I was not embracing the new math—Divine Math. It doesn't have to add up when God is in the mix. He created math, after all. He certainly knows a few formulas that we haven't come up with yet. Just ask Moses how he was going to provide meat for the Israelites to eat for a month in the desert. The numbers simply did not add up. Ask Noah how this boat in the desert was going to save his family from a flood that no one else believed would come. Ask him how much food he would need to feed everyone, human and animal, on that boat for . . . yeah, ask him how long the trip was going to be. There are a lot of things that do not add up in the Bible.

I am working hard at embracing the new Divine Math. I am learning to rejoice in what He has promised to do, even if at the moment I do not see it. You would think by now I would have figured this new math thing out. God has demonstrated it in my life so many times. When I first stepped out of ministry from my first full-time call, just months after having purchased our first home, God was faithful to provide more than we needed.

When we left the new jobs God had provided for Shirley and me, in order to return to the parish for a very substantial pay cut, God provided more than we needed. When we packed up our young family and moved from Minnesota to Texas into a home someone else picked out for us, God provided more than we needed. When we chose to adopt a son with special needs that would challenge him and us for many years, God provided more than we needed. And the list goes on . . .

So, I am giving you permission to remind me about how this new math works. I am reminding myself of the calling we received and of the faithfulness of God to provide. Sometimes I forget to notice we are still in our home. We still both have jobs outside of GodPonders that are helping with the expenses. We do have speaking dates on our calendar. We do have a multitude of amazing friends who have continued to encourage and support us. And we have a God who sees where we are going, as well as where we are at. Not only does God see our future story, He has written the script.

Praise be to our faithful God!

SOMETHING TO PONDER:
When has God worked new math in your life?

CAN YOU HEAR ME NOW?

Listen, my son, and be wise, and keep your heart on the right path.
Proverbs 23:19 (NIV)

In a stroke of great advertising, Verizon came up with a series of commercials a few years ago that asked the question, "Can you hear me now?" These ads were designed to show us how great their coverage was; you could take your call anywhere.

I must admit, in our new home I find myself asking people the same question from time to time when I am on my cell phone. It seems our home is in a small valley, which makes cell coverage less than optimal. It is very frustrating to hear only part of a conversation, or to only have some of your words go through. These are the conversations that rumors are made from.

I have also found that, in my "midlife," my hearing is not what it was a few years ago. At a table full of people with multiple conversations going on around me, I struggle to pick out any single conversation. But I have learned to cope—lots of smiling and nodding!

I have no idea what it must have been like for the gentleman who was brought by his friends to Jesus for healing. Mark records he "was deaf and could barely talk." This is a far cry from dropped words, or hearing too many conversations at once. This is a world of silence and minimal communication. His friends "begged Jesus to place his hand on the man." Jesus took the friend away from the ever-present crowd, and put His fingers in the man's ears. Jesus then spit and touched the man's tongue.

Jesus looked toward heaven and let out a deep sigh. Then, recorded in Jesus' own native tongue, He says, "Ephphatha" (which means "Be opened!"). With a single command from the lips of Jesus, the man's ears were opened and his tongue was free to speak. This action amazed those who witnessed the change. They said, "He has done everything well, He even makes the deaf to hear and the mute to speak."

> *Then will the eyes of the blind be opened and the ears of the deaf unstopped.*
> *Then will the lame leap like a deer, and the mute tongue shout for joy.*
> *Water will gush forth in the wilderness and streams in the desert.*
> (Isaiah 35:5, 6 NIV)

One simple command of Jesus, "Be Opened," reveals for me the very deepest cry of the gospel. The cry that we might truly hear, and clearly speak. There are many days when I know that that Lord is really saying to me, "Can you hear me now?"

At lunch recently, I shared with a good friend of mine the struggle I was having hearing from the Lord as I seek His will for my future. The next several moments were spent recalling what had been happening in my life in the last few months. My friend didn't say a word, but just let me share my experiences, and my frustration of waiting on God. After listening to me, he just smiled and with a chuckle asked, "So how loud does the Lord have to shout for you to hear Him?"

I was blessed over the next few days after our lunch, to hear from the Lord with such clarity that it was frightening. I was also reminded, as

I pondered my friend's words, that I am in good company. God shouted at a lot of people to get their attention; from Abraham to Paul, the Bible is full of accounts of our shouting God. Scripture is also filled with people filled with fear at the very Word of the Lord.

I pray that I continue to listen, being careful to discern His voice, and then listen some more. I know that His voice will continue to challenge me to clearly speak the gospel. My prayer is that you, too, would be listening, and hearing from our loving God as He speaks to you. Then you can stand with me, and the unnumbered others who have stood in amazement and declared, "He has done everything well, He even makes the deaf hear and the mute speak."

SOMETHING TO PONDER:

How have you heard God speak to you in the past? What are you listening for Him to say today?

WHICH WAY WOULD YOU RUN?

And pray in the Spirit on all occasions with all kinds of prayers and requests.
With this in mind, be alert and always keep on praying for all the saints.
Ephesians 6:18 (NIV)

While there are many people with the goal of running a marathon on their bucket list, let me assure you, it is not on mine. Nor is a half marathon, a 5k race, or the cross-the-parking-lot scramble. While I have been known to do a quick sprint or two, any real distance is not on my horizon.

Back in the day, when my wife and I managed a group home for at-risk youth, we would occasionally have a youth decide they no longer wanted to live with us, regardless of what the courts said. When this happened, they would often simply run away. I was known to chase a runaway or two . . . I even caught them. In fact, I overheard a conversation between two boys one night when a new member of the house was given this advice, "Don't try and run when Mr. McCourt is working—he might actually catch you."

These days, however, I have a hard and fast rule about running: run only if being chased, and only if you think you can get away. So far, this rule has served me well. For those who do not share this rule, but who actually enjoy running, many of them set their sights on one particular marathon.

The Boston Marathon: a day all about running, attended by thousands of dedicated runners, has become a worldwide iconic event. The 2013 race was no exception. Runners and press from around the world were at the marathon. Thousands more gathered as spectators. Some were Bostonians, family friends, and sports fanatics. The sidelines were also scattered with police, EMTs, firefighters, and other first responders. They were there to help if needed, and to keep the runners and the spectators safe. This marathon was different; it is remembered for runners, but runners of a different kind.

I remember the day well. I jumped into my car after work for the short drive home. I was stunned by the news on the radio: a bombing at the Boston Marathon. I got home and heard more news, and began to see images from the attack on the TV and Internet. I was struck by the runners, thousands of them, running in different directions. There were the runners who were running down the middle of the street toward the finish line as the explosions occurred. There were people in the moments after the explosions running to get away, and to get to a place they perceived as safe.

But my attention was drawn to the runners running into the smoke, running toward the explosion sites. There we found police, the EMTs, the firefighters, and the other first responders. There were still others, they were the marathon runners, the bystanders, the loved ones. Some were doctors, or nurses, and some were not running because of any expertise they had, they were simply running to provide whatever help they could offer.

As I watched the photos and the videos, I began to ask myself, "Which way would you run?" While I would like to think I would be found among those who ran to help, and I pray that I would, any answer I could give would only be speculation. I thought of other runners I have read about. About the father who runs to embrace his wayward, returning son (The Prodigal Son—Luke 15:11-32). I also thought of the women who ran from and the disciples who ran to the tomb of Jesus on that Easter morning (The Resurrection—John 20:1-9). I also thought of the millions of saints who, upon their entrance to heaven, must run with great joy to the throne.

As I was pondering the events of that day in 2013, I came upon the photo of a true hero, someone who ran into the heart of the battle that day, who did not run or turn away from the need that was present. She ran as fast as her aged knees would carry her, but she didn't run to help a single victim she saw, or to fetch a bandage or water. She ran straight to the throne of God. In the middle of the chaos all around her, she dropped to her knees, frightened, perplexed, confused, and perhaps angered. She went to the One who does not grow tired or weary, to the One who is life amidst a tragedy. I don't know her name, but her witness has been seen around the world. I think that she ran the right way.

SOMETHING TO PONDER:
What sends you running to the throne room of God?

JESUS LOVES YOU . . . BUT I'M HIS FAVORITE

The LORD appeared to us in the past, saying: "I have loved you with an everlasting love; I have drawn you with loving-kindness."
Jeremiah 31:3 (NIV)

R ight from the start, let me confess this title is not original. I found this saying some years ago on a drink coaster. It was in a collection of humorous sayings, and I did find it humorous enough to buy it. After looking at it for many months (it was on my desk in my office), I discovered that behind the humor was a deeply profound theological truth.

In my relationship with my Heavenly Father, I am His favorite. Being a perfect Father, He loves all His children the same—we are all His favorites. This might seem a bit trite, especially in light of the fact that our American culture has told us we are all special—which, translated, means none of us are special. To view yourself as one of God's favorites, to me, changes my relationship with Him. It softens for me any fear I have of approaching Him with anything. It boosts my self-esteem (my Christ-esteem), and it also emboldens me to share the amazing truth with others: "God loves you, but I'm His favorite." I don't, however, stop there; I usually, after a brief pause, add "but don't worry—you're His favorite, too."

Need some proof that you are His favorite?

You see, at just the right time, when we were still powerless, Christ died for the ungodly. Very rarely will anyone die for a righteous man, though for a good man someone might possibly dare to die. But God demonstrates his own love for us in this: While we were still sinners, Christ died for us.
Romans 5:6-8

I know how challenging it can be to serve people who have offended me in some way. Paul's words were so clear when he speaks of God's amazing demonstration of love, the very sacrifice of His Son for me while I was yet a sinner.

The Lord appeared to us in the past, saying: "I have loved you with an everlasting love; I have drawn you with loving-kindness.
Jeremiah 31:3

Are not five sparrows sold for two pennies? Yet not one of them is forgotten by God. Indeed, the very hairs of your head are all numbered. Don't be afraid; you are worth more than many sparrows.
Luke 12:6-7

To know that God knows the very number of the hairs on my head (which is diminishing by the day) speaks to me of His intimate knowledge of me. To even care enough to know the numbers of the hairs on my head is an overwhelming thought. God's Word also reminds me that He knows my name. Have you ever watched the face of a child light up when you call them by name? I have witnessed this time and time again over years of ministry, for Shirley works hard to learn the names of children we minister to.

For me, the best proof of His love for me is found in Jesus' explanation to Nicodemus of the reality of the Kingdom of God and our rebirth in the Spirit.

"For God so loved the world that he gave his one and only Son, that whoever believes in him shall not perish but have eternal life."
John 3:16

Go ahead and pass it on: "Jesus Loves You . . . But I'm His Favorite. And So Are You!"

SOMETHING TO PONDER:
Who do you know who needs to hear that they are God's favorite?

DO YOU HAVE A THIRD?

As iron sharpens iron, so one man sharpens another.
Proverbs 27:17

This journey we call life can be challenging, difficult, and frustrating—and that's on a good day.

I have been very blessed to have faithful men of God around me over the years. These men have come from various churches, backgrounds, and age groups, but they have all been a blessing in my life. With these men I have studied the Word of God, prayed for the needs of others, and had amazing fellowship.

But today I'm not talking about surrounding ourselves with men and women of integrity, as important as that is. I am talking about my third relationship, after my relationship with Christ (which comes first), and after my relationship with my family (which comes second). Do you know what it is? Trust me, if you have it, you know exactly what I am talking about. If you think the answer is "work," we need to talk again soon.

The third relationship I am talking about is a close and trusted Christian brother or sister (brother for brother, and sister for sister—just so we are clear on this) who knows who you are behind the mask. This is someone who knows your deepest struggles, and your greatest joys. He or she knows when you fall and will help you up. This person is someone who, despite all they know about you, still loves you with the love of Christ. In this relationship, you are both that "third" for each other. This person also is the first to get in your face when they see you headed where you should not be going, and will even say what you don't want to hear.

In Christian circles, we call this person an accountability person—and they are—but there is also more to the relationship. I've already told you that I have been blessed with faithful godly men in my life, too many to even name. I rejoice over each and every one of them and know that I have grown through my relationships with them. In my fifty years of living, I have had only one true "third."

This man in my life is a man I have known now for more than fifteen years. I have not been an "Iron-sharpens-Iron" type of confidant and prayer warrior with him for all these years, but for many of them. This is not a relationship that came in an instant; it grew over time— much time. I am doubly blessed that our wives share a relationship as well (talk about accountability!).

As with all of my GodPonders, this idea is not original.

> *A friend loves at all times, and a brother is born for adversity.*
> Proverbs 17:17

> *A man of many companions may come to ruin, but there is a friend who sticks closer than a brother.*
> Proverbs 18:24

The more I walk through life, the more I am convinced that my heart's desire for my boys, and my wife, is to find a "third" relationship in their life and maintain it. It has also long been my prayer for the youth I have worked with for more than 25 years, that they would find one solid Christian friend.

I pray that you find such a friend, and I rejoice in mine. Thanks, Nick!

SOMETHING TO PONDER:
Do you have a third in your life? If not, how can you develop that relationship?

ARE YOU TALKING TO ME?

Let the wise listen and add to their learning, and let the discerning get guidance.
Proverbs 1:5 (NIV)

I grew up as the youngest of four boys. I can recall many times when my brothers and I would be watching TV together and my dad would come in and tell us to get ready for dinner. He would walk away and his message would go unheeded. It was not that we did not hear him. I'm sure, in most cases, we all heard him. A few minutes later, he would come in the room again and he would see that we had not moved at all. This time he would step in front of the TV, after shutting it off, and ask why we were not at the table. Our individual response: "Are you talking to me?"

In our defense, there were four of us in there—he should have been more specific. After all, it was not like we all sat down for dinner together. No, wait . . . I guess we did always all sit down to dinner together. There have even been times as a parent when I would enter a room, and tell something to the only child in the room, and after I had repeated myself several times they would say, "Are you talking to me?"

As I work my way through the Bible, I am again reminded of just how often God's people must have said, "Are you talking to me?" When Nathan went to David and confronted him with his sin, I am sure that David's immediate reaction was, "Are you talking to me?" David figured out quickly that Nathan was, in fact, talking to him. I'm sure that the initial reaction of Moses to a talking bush was, "Are you talking to me?" I'm sure that Abram, when told to take his family and go to a land unknown, might have said, "Are you talking to me?"

This is not just an Old Testament thought. When Joseph was greeted in a dream and told about the child to be born of Mary, he probably said, "Are you talking to me?" The shepherds that first Christmas night, at the appearance of the angel, must have asked, "Are you talking to me?" (Although, I imagine that once the sky filled with more angels, they got the point.)

The religious leaders, when listening to Jesus, had a little different take on the question. They may have said, "You're not talking to me." Luke, in the book of Acts, recorded the account of Saul's conversion. Sent out on a mission to find and persecute more Christians, Saul was struck blind by Jesus. Ananias, who had heard all about Saul, was then asked by the Lord to go and visit Saul. You know, the guy who was out to get all the believers! Listen to these words and I'm sure you will hear Ananias, in good Bible-speak, say, "Are you talking to me?"

> *The Lord told him, "Go to the house of Judas on Straight Street and ask for a man from Tarsus named Saul, for he is praying. In a vision he has seen a man named Ananias come and place his hands on him to restore his sight." "Lord," Ananias answered, "I have heard many reports about this man and all the harm he has done to your holy people in Jerusalem. And he has come here with authority from the chief priests to arrest all who call on your name."*
>
> (Did you hear it—"Are you talking to me?")
>
> *But the Lord said to Ananias, "Go! This man is my chosen instrument to proclaim my name to the Gentiles and their kings and to the people of Israel.*
>
> Acts 9:11-14

Ananias, Abram, the shepherds, Moses, David, Peter, Jonah, and a host of others through the ages have been called to do things that seemed impossible. There have been times when God's people have even asked to see God's I.D. so they could confirm who was talking to them. Does this ever happen to you?

Today, I want to encourage you to read scripture with the question in mind: "Are you talking to me?" Just so we are all on the same page, the answer to the question is YES He is!

- When God calls us to lay down our life and take up our cross, *He's talking to you.* (Luke 9:23)
- When He tells us to go make disciples of all nations, *He's talking to you.* (Matthew 28:18-20)
- When He says that He forgives all our sins and declares us righteous, *He's talking to you.* (1 Peter 2:24)
- When He promises that He will never leave or forsake us, *He's talking to you.* (Deuteronomy 31:6)
- When He tells us about eternal life, *He's talking to you.* (John 11:25)

I would even challenge yourself to ask the question out loud. The next time you are in Starbucks, reading the Bible, stop and look around and say out loud, "Are you talking to me?" After a brief ponder, announce out loud, "Yep, He's talking to me." Not only will it give you a new look at the Word, but the lady at the next table will give you a look that opens the door to share the gospel with her.

SOMETHING TO PONDER:
What has God said to you through His Word that made you ask, "Are you talking to me?"

WAITING: A LOST ART

Wait for the LORD; be strong and take heart and wait for the LORD.
Psalm 27:14 (NIV)

Not long ago, I was sitting in the second floor waiting room at Bobby and Steve's Auto World. I had stopped in to get the oil changed in my van. When I was at the check-in counter, the gentleman mentioned that I could help myself to fountain drinks or coffee. He then explained that I could go upstairs and connect to the free Wi-Fi. He said he would call me on the PA when my wait was over.

Filled with leather couches, the waiting room also boasted a gas fireplace, a pinball machine, tables and chairs, a patio deck, and even a sofa made from the back end of a classic car, where I was sitting. All of this was designed to help me wait. I may just start going there to hang out with my laptop and a 64oz coffee.

Waiting is a lost art. We live in such an instant world that we don't know how to wait. We even design rooms to help us forget that we are waiting. Don't believe me? Let's look at a few other examples. We have gone way past the telephone to "instant messaging," which now is more like nonstop messaging. We can't wait for the nightly news, we need it 24 hours a day. We even have Taco Bell Express; after all, the wait at Taco Bell is sometimes too long! Disney has spent millions of dollars to develop a series of slowly-moving lines with entertainment along the way, so you forget the three-hour wait for the four-minute ride. They've even gone further to create a FastPass system, which you can acquire so you can bypass the entertaining queue altogether!

We don't wait for a chance to get to the store to buy new music. We hear it on the radio, click a button, buy it, and download it to our personal data universe. The online retailer Amazon, which began as an online book store with crazy-fast mail delivery, now carries anything you might need, and lots that you don't. Now when a friend starts telling us about a great book they read, we can have it delivered to our e-reader before they finish telling us why they liked it.

Overnight film developing and printing was reduced to 1-hour photo processing—no wait, that was shortened to instant print kiosks at the local grocery store . . . now we can simply take the photo anywhere with our phone, post it to Facebook automatically, and send it to our photo printer at home so the photo will be waiting for us when we get home.

Parents today struggle to teach their children how to wait—whether for a desired toy, or a computer game—because we as parents do not know how to wait, either. This is a danger that leads not only to materialism but also to great spiritual distress. The journey of faith is not an instant walk. It is a journey filled with waiting, learning, stumbling, rising, waiting again, and finding joy in the journey.

This inability to wait is causing issues in the lives of many Christian adults today. We are not willing to wait; we want God to answer our prayer *right now*. We want the pain and the struggle to end by morning. But, to a God whose origins are from eternity, His view of time is very different from ours. God, who is able to create in a moment, and heal in an instant, also knows that it is often through the waiting that we grow. The account of God's people is filled with waiting: Abraham for a child, Noah for dry ground, Job for understanding, and all the children of Israel for their Messiah.

Today, so many have begun to see the period of waiting as God's inability, or lack of desire, to help. In their impatience they question God, or they take matters into their own hands. This leads to their folly and diminishes our witness of God's faithfulness to our world.

The psalmist understood the wait, and the blessings to follow:

> *Wait for the Lord; be strong and take heart and wait for the Lord.*
> Psalm 27:14

> *We wait in hope for the Lord; he is our help and our shield.*
> Psalm 33:20

> *Be still before the Lord and wait patiently for him; do not fret when men succeed in their ways, when they carry out their wicked schemes.*
> Psalm 37:7

> *I wait for you, O Lord; you will answer, O Lord my God.*
> Psalm 38:15

> *I waited patiently for the Lord; he turned to me and heard my cry.*
> Psalm 40:1

I have experienced the joy of holy waiting. The blessing to see that the waiting was not in vain, but for my own good.

Next time you need to "wait" for anything, say a quick prayer of thanks to God for the chance to slow down, and remind yourself of the blessing of holy waiting.

But they who wait for the Lord shall renew their strength; they shall mount up with wings like eagles; they shall run and not be weary; they shall walk and not faint.
Isaiah 40:31

See you in the waiting room!

SOMETHING TO PONDER:
When do you least enjoy waiting? Are you waiting on God for anything right now?

POWER OUTAGE

Let your light shine before men,
that they may see your good deeds and praise your Father in heaven.
Matthew 5:16 (NIV)

It seems like the Midwest gets hit by a series of severe thunderstorms every spring. The resulting storms often leave trees down, roads flooded, and basements wet.

Not too long ago, one such storm left 250,000+ homes without electricity. Many of these homes were without electricity for more than a week. One of the homes without electricity was my youngest son's home. He lived just fifteen minutes from us, so I drove over to his home and packed up food from his freezer. I brought all the food home to my freezer to keep it frozen until they had power again. Wouldn't you? Let's face it—if you had freezer space and could help your friend during a power outage, you would do it.

On my way to my son's home, I heard the hum of generators that were sitting in many driveways. I also noticed the power cords running inside the doors. These cords no doubt ran freezers, sump pumps, and maybe a lamp or two.

The scene reminded me of a storm that hit my home a few years earlier when we were living in Waconia, MN. I woke up one morning to the sound of what I believed to be lawn mowers. I soon discovered that they were generators. The neighbors had noticed what I had not: our power was out. What happened next still amazes me.

We had about four generators in the cul de sac, with cords running everywhere. They ran across the road, over lawns, and through flower beds. The power for my sump pump came from a generator across the street, the power for my freezer came from a generator next door. Everyone was sharing their power with one another. Wouldn't you?

So what about the storms of life that our friends and neighbors get caught in? Storms of job loss or illness, the winds of depression or addictions, a sudden flood of unexpected expenses. What do we do when we see a coworker or friend who is without power? Someone who is trying to cope on their own? Are we willing to fire up the generator and run a power cord over to them?

Are we willing to share the love of Christ with them? Are we willing to tell them about the unending power supplied to us at our weakest point? Are we willing to just sit with them in the dark until the lights turn back on in their world?

> *But he said to me, "My grace is sufficient for you, for my power is made perfect in weakness." Therefore I will boast all the more gladly about my weaknesses, so that Christ's power may rest on me.*
> 2 Corinthians 12:9 (NIV)

We have a God who, even at His weakest, is stronger than any of us.

> *For the foolishness of God is wiser than man's wisdom, and the weakness of God is stronger than man's strength.*
> 1 Corinthians 1:25 (NIV)

Jesus called us the light of the world. We live in the darkness of a world without power, called to shine the light of Christ. This light shows them how great their need is and allows them to see Him for who He is. As one who gets caught in the dark storms of depression from time to time, I know the amazing grace of a friend with a lamp.

You are the light of the world. A city on a hill cannot be hidden.
Matthew 5:14 (NIV)

Let's grab a power cord and head out into the neighborhood. After all, we were not left in the dark alone.

But you are a chosen people, a royal priesthood, a holy nation, a people belonging to God, that you may declare the praises of him who called you out of darkness into his wonderful light.
1 Peter 2:9 (NIV)

SOMETHING TO PONDER:
Who do you know that is caught in a power outage? What action and word can bring light into their life?

HIS CALLING IS BETTER THAN MY BUCKET LIST

As the heavens are higher than the earth, so are my ways higher than your ways and my thoughts than your thoughts.
Isaiah 55:9 (NIV)

I am a UthGuy (pronounced YouthGuy) who has been working in youth ministry for more than 25 years. Above that I have built a series of hopes and aspirations, a sort of career "bucket list." I am happy to report that many of these items have been fulfilled. There are a few, however, that have hung on for a long time, and have even caused some frustration and disappointment.

As yet another National Youth Gathering for the LCMS comes into focus, and my 50th birthday grows fuzzy in the rear-view mirror, I realize that one of the items on my bucket list—"Speak at a National Youth Gathering"—fades yet again. I have to admit with some embarrassment that I have shared this desire with very few—until today, that is. I have even re-written this paragraph several times to see if I could leave the specifics out and keep the message intact . . . didn't work, as you can tell.

As I have continued my personal journey through Mark's Gospel, I came across someone else who was disappointed. He is known to many as the "man of the tombs," a man filled with an evil spirit who was forced to live alone in the tombs. They had tried over the years to restrain him with ropes, even chains, but he could not be bound. All day and night he would wander through the tombs, cutting himself with rocks and crying out.

One day, Jesus come to his region, and he ran to Him and fell on his knees. Jesus had told the spirit to come out of him. At this, the wild man from the tombs shouted at Jesus, "What do you want with me, Jesus, Son of the Most High God? Swear to God that you won't torture me!"

Then Jesus asked him, "What is your name?" "My name is Legion," he replied, "for we are many." And he begged Jesus again and again not to send them out of the area. A large herd of pigs was feeding on the nearby hillside. The demons begged Jesus, "Send us among the pigs; allow us to go into them." He gave them permission, and the evil spirits came out and went into the pigs. The herd, about two thousand in number, rushed down the steep bank into the lake and were drowned.

Those tending the pigs ran off and reported this in the town and countryside, and the people went out to see what had happened. When they came to Jesus, they saw the man who had been possessed by the legion of demons, sitting there, dressed and in his right mind; and they were afraid. Those who had seen it told the people what had happened to the demon-possessed man—and told about the pigs as well. Then the people began to plead with Jesus to leave their region.

As Jesus was getting into the boat, the man who had been demon-possessed begged to go with him. Jesus did not let him, but said, "Go home to your family and tell them how much the Lord has done for you, and how he has had mercy on you." So the man went away and began to tell in the Decapolis how much Jesus had done for him. And all the people were amazed.
Mark 5:11-20 (NIV)

What a day . . . I am sure it started like any other—awakening cold and sore, alone among the tombs. Then Jesus arrived. The demons, who were in control, ran toward Jesus in attack mode. Upon arrival at Jesus' feet, the demons ended up begging for mercy from Him. Driven away in a dramatic, suicidal pig stampede, the man was left behind. But this time he was not alone; he was among friends. He was clothed by them and, for the first time in a long time, he was then in control of himself.

I am guessing he never saw the events of that day coming. This man of the tombs may well have resigned himself to his fate. Then everything was made new by the love and authority of Jesus. The man of the tombs had but one request: "the man who had been demon-possessed begged to go with him." The people of the region were not too happy with Jesus—He frightened them, and He was upsetting their world. I can imagine that this man got more than a few hostile looks from the crowd. I would even speculate that he wondered if the community would welcome him back. A new item was added to this man's bucket list: his desire to travel with Jesus—to be an amazing witness to what Jesus had done.

But it was not to be. Jesus did not let him, but said, "Go home to your family and tell them how much the Lord has done for you, and how he has had mercy on you." (Mark 5:19) The man of the tombs, with a story that lived 2,000-some years after the event, was sent to a small audience—his family. What a great place to start—who better to see and understand the amazing transformation that had taken place? It is an amazing account that will be passed on for generations. "And all the people were amazed."

As I read this account, I have discovered a renewed calling for me: "Go home to your family and tell them how much the Lord has done for you, and how he has had mercy on you." My bucket list is just that—it's mine. I am slowly learning to yield my short-sighted, often self-centered bucket list to the One whose vision is eternal and desires nothing but the best for me!

While we are on the subject of lists, I have something you can add to your "to do" list: "Remind Craig of the amazing calling of God placed on his life to go and tell his family."

I am blessed, you know, with a huge family—both by birth and by the God who calls His people together to be family.

SOMETHING TO PONDER
Is there something in your life, on your "Bucket List" that you need to yield to God?

A BONUS PONDER

WELCOME, FATHER

By Shirley McCourt

WELCOME, FATHER

"For the Lord is good; his steadfast love endures forever,
and his faithfulness to all generations."
Psalm 100:5

It was a cool but pleasant March day, the promise of spring in the air. My husband, Craig, and I got out of the car and walked up to the house. I lagged behind, taking deep breaths in an effort to maintain my composure, but emotions threatened to spill over as we prepared to meet our new son for the first time.

As Craig neared the house, the door opened and a little boy we had never met opened the door and said, "Welcome, Father!" Yes, you read that correctly. We were meeting our seven-year-old son (who we legally adopted one year later) for the first time.

Needless to say, those brimming emotions did indeed spill over as a few tears ran down my cheeks. Any doubts we had, that this adventure we had embarked on was not God's will, were gone. My heavenly Father used the words of this little boy to assure me He was present in this adoption. My son got it right—the man walking up to the house was his father.

Much time has passed since that March day in 2001. We have had more joy, love, and laughter—but not all days have been that way. Thinking about that day, however, reminds me of two of the lessons I have gleaned over the years. One is God's incredible faithfulness. When I say not all days have been the joy-filled kind, it is an understatement. We have had conflict, frustration, anger, mistakes, and lots more tears spilling over. There have been days of chaos and uncertainty, but the one constant has been God's faithfulness.

He has been faithful in surrounding us with an amazing group of people to support our family. He has given us friends to take our boys fishing, pray with us, welcome every part of us into their homes, and even cry with us at times. He has given us wonderful case managers, county workers, and therapists in a vast array of specialties that worked with our son and with us. To this day, we remain friends with camp workers, teachers, and care attendants that encouraged our son in ways we could not. When a little space was necessary to maintain our relationship with our son, He gave us respite workers and foster families. Our adopted son has grown into a compassionate, committed, and intelligent young man who is passionate about the causes he believes in. He has learned to manage his disability and excel in ways no one imagined when he was seven.

God has been faithful with our older, biological son as well. The love and compassion God created in him made it possible for us to adopt a child on the Autism Spectrum. The patience he showed when Mom and Dad had to deal with difficult situations can only be attributed to the Fruit of the Spirit in him. He, too, has grown into a kind, loyal, and intelligent young man who loves God's outdoor creation. He is committed to our family and a hard worker.

We had laughter when we wanted to fling ourselves on the bed in despair, and joy in seeing our sons horseplay together or conspire to surprise Mom with one of those Mother's Day breakfasts that inspires those words, "Wow, you really were creative and worked hard on this!" God's faithfulness was also made known to us in our finances. A gift, bonus, or new funding stream came just when a bill needed to be paid or a therapy aid needed to be purchased.

Our families supported us when so many extended families question or complain about decisions that have to be made. We were able to find ways to take vacations and go on family mission trips that have given us memories to cherish forever. Our churches and employers were flexible with time and schedules. We have discovered that many relationships between husband and wife become strained, or even broken, when raising a child with special needs. By God's grace and faithfulness, Craig and I have found ways to resolve conflict, encourage one another, and stay united as one in Christ.

All of these examples—and the many that I cannot put into words—point us to our Father God and His faithfulness. Our experience is a testament to God's Word:

> *"For the Lord is good; his steadfast love endures forever, and his faithfulness to all generations."*
> Psalm 100:5 (NIV)

Yes, there have been challenges over the years, but we have learned much since that memorable spring day when we met our son for the first time. Which brings to mind the second lesson I mentioned. As I think about my son saying, "Welcome, Father," I am reminded of my relationship with my Heavenly Father.

How often I say, "Welcome, Father" with the excitement of abundance and good times bolstering me. I thrill that God's Spirit lives in me through my baptism, the Lord's Supper, and God's Word, and smile at how good God is. However, when things are not so peachy, I try once again (just like my son) to do things on my own. "Welcome, Father" does not come so quickly to my lips. My smile is less frequent and I question God's timing.

But God is always faithful and is waiting for me, just as the Father waited for the Prodigal Son, to once again turn to Him in repentance and trust. He is faithful to forgive, faithful to bless, and faithful to grow the Fruit of the Spirit in me. I will hold fast to God's Word:

Let us hold unswervingly to the hope we profess, for he who promised is faithful.
Hebrews 10:23 (NIV)

SOMETHING TO PONDER:
Looking back, what is an difficult experience in which you can now see God's faithfulness?

ABOUT GODPONDERS

Pondering God, Proclaiming Christ

They will proclaim the works of God and ponder what he has done.
Psalm 64:9 (NIV)

As disciples of Christ, we seek to use the stories of scripture and life to proclaim the works of God, and ponder what He has done, encouraging and equipping others to do the same.

Craig is a Certified Lay Minister in the LCMS with more than 25 years of full-time parish experience. He brings a high level of energy and humor whenever he speaks. Craig's passion to share Christ's awesome power and presence, together with his ability to hold the attention of an audience from Junior High through adults, makes him a great choice for any conference, camp, dinner, seminar, or for a variety of other events.

Shirley is a Certified DCE in the LCMS. Her passion is to help women develop a deeper relationship with Jesus Christ and grow in their love of scripture. Her joy and love for her Lord is seen as she leads retreats, Bible studies, and workshops.

WHAT OTHERS ARE SAYING

"Craig McCourt is one of the most inspiring, yet down-to-earth speakers I have ever had the opportunity to listen to. His God-given talents are many. I particularly like the fact that Craig is extremely effective in motivating and uplifting people of all age groups—teens, parents, seniors—with his love for the Lord. Craig is also exceptional at getting people to see that God has created and Called each and every one of us for a special purpose. Craig's center remains his faith in Jesus Christ. Everyone who hears him speak and share will be touched by Jesus and Craig's passion for the Great Commission. And he'll even make you laugh too."

Dr. Jim Pingel
Dept. Chair—Concordia University, Wisconsin

"Craig has been blessed by God with the gift of speaking. He is engaging, easy to listen to, and hilarious. Not only has God given him the ability to be a great speaker, but God has equipped Craig with crazy and true life stories. You will be amazed at all the things that he has experienced in his life. It is evident that these stories are not just for entertainment, but they are meant to show God at work in our world. It is easy to take Craig's message and make personal applications. Craig's messages are personal, powerful, relevant, and unforgettable. His messages have meaning long after the speaking event is over. Inspiring!"

Becky Puckett
Teacher—Trinity Lutheran School, Waconia, MN

"I have heard Craig McCourt speak on many occasions in varied venues, to young and old, formal and informal settings, in a classroom, behind a podium and on a stage, in costume or in a suit and tie. Whatever the forum, whatever the topic, Craig's ability to connect with his audience and creatively convey his message leaves you smiling, pondering, wiser and moved. He truly has a gift of speaking and a heart for the Lord."

Melanie Haubrich
Owner—Haubrich Design, Waconia, MN

"This guy is a funny, funny man"

Rev. Dr. Jeffery Schrank
Pastor—Christ Church Lutheran, Phoenix, AZ

. . . AND STILL OTHERS

"If you are in need of a speaker with bold enthusiasm, who is clear and to the point, I would recommend Craig McCourt for a Sunday service or special event. He is very able to communicate clearly the great Gospel message in sermon or topic format. He is very comfortable as a preacher and presenter. Both my wife and I have enjoyed his sermons very much when we have had occasion to be present."

Rev. Layton L. Lemke, Emeritus
Norwood Young America, MN

"I have heard Craig McCourt preach, teach, and talk on numerous occasions. He is an excellent communicator and presenter for all age levels, and uses a style that is engaging, relevant, and inspiring. He is also adept at using humor to communicate points and make them more memorable. Based on my experience, Craig's message will not disappoint you."

Dan Haupt
Director of Operations—The Alley, Cottage Grove, MN

"Craig is a dynamic speaker who has experienced life. He's witty, humorous, and very well connected with all age groups."

Jim Strehlke
Teacher—Lutheran High School, Mayer, MN

"I have known Craig since the mid '90s. He is a an excellent communicator with just the right mix of humor and facts. I have seen Craig speak before small medium and large sized groups and he holds the attention of them all. Best of all, I have seen firsthand that youth and adults leave his presentations wanting more. If you are looking for an entertaining and dynamic speaker, I would highly recommend him."

Nick Rogosienski
Local Sales Manager—CarSoup.com, Minneapolis, MN

"Few speakers have the unique ability to make you laugh and cry at the same time. Craig uses this gift to tear down our defenses and open our hearts to the Truth."

John Ingelin
Head writer—Creation Files

DISCOVER MORE ONLINE

www.GodPonders.org
www.CraigMcCourt.com

 @Craigmccourt

 /GodPonders

CHANGING LIVES

There are many experiences that have shaped our lives and the lives of our children, and our congregations. If you are looking for intentional change, transformational change toward the servant heart of Jesus we can think of no better way than through a short term mission trip.

We also think a great organization to work with from logistics to missional training and development is World Servants. We serve with and highly recommend World Servants. Join us sometime on a family mission trip.

<>< Craig & Shirley McCourt

As for me and my mouse we will serve the Lord.

Above all else, guard your heart,
for it is the wellspring of life.
Proverbs 4:23 (NIV)

GodPonders.org

DEVOTIONAL / BIBLE STUDY FOR MEN

*Mouse Pads currently available through GodPonders.org

NEED A SPEAKER?

Why not invite Craig or Shirley to your next conference or congregational event. To find out more about bringing Craig or Shirley to your event, or to check their current speaking schedule visit www.GodPonders.org.

HERE ARE JUST A COUPLE TOPICS TO PONDER

I'm Not Normal

I've spent the better part of 50 years trying to fit in, to be part of those who are normal, only to come to the startling conclusion *there is no such thing as normal*. In Scripture we are called: "Peculiar People", "Sheep", "Royal", "Adopted", "Born Again", "Hand Made", Light", and "Salt" just to name a few. Take and entertaining and insightful look at the fact that there is no such thing as normal, while discovering who God has uniquely created you to be.

Breathe

Since the fall in the garden, satan, the world, and even our own foolish choices seek to "knock the wind out of us." Let's look at what it means to have the breath of God in us and how to live the "breath-taking" life God has for us.

PLANNING A RETREAT?

Did you know that GodPonders does
retreats? With a background in camp
Ministry Shirley enjoys helping groups
grow in their relationship with Christ. .
To find out more about bringing Craig
or Shirley to your retreat, or to check
their current speaking schedule visit
www.GodPonders.org.

HERE ARE JUST A COUPLE TOPICS TO PONDER

Crafted by The King

As women we sometimes feel bruised or even broken. God sees us
as His beloved children. Discover some of the words God uses to
describe you and how He equips you to serve Him with confidence
and joy. This retreat works very well as a crafting/quilting retreat
with an added spiritual dimension.

This I Know

"Jesus loves me. This I know…" is the basis for this retreat. In a
world filled with uncertainty, God's Word remains certain. This
retreat helps us focus on what we know about God and how He
works in our lives. It moves us from a place of questioning the
difficulties to better focusing on the absolute truth of God in our
lives.

Made in the USA
Middletown, DE
23 June 2015